Subduction Zone

Subduction Zone

Emily McGiffin

PEDLAR PRESS

ST JOHN'S

ACKNOWLEDGEMENTS
The publisher wishes to thank the Canada
Council for the Arts and the NL Publishers
Assistance Program for their generous
support of our publishing program.

LIBRARY AND ARCHIVES CANADA
CATALOGUING IN PUBLICATION

McGiffin, Emily, 1980-, author
    Subduction zone / Emily McGiffin.

ISBN 978-1-897141-66-3 (pbk.)

    I. Title.

PS8625.G52S92 2014   C811'.6
C2014-904670-7

COVER ART & ILLUSTRATIONS
Erica Gajewski

DESIGN
Zab Design & Typography, Toronto

TYPEFACE
Cardea (Emigre) by David Cabianca

Printed in Canada

No pidamos milagros, no pidamos que se interese
por el bien del país quien viene como extranjero
para hacer su fortuna y marcharse después.

— JOSÉ RIZAL

CONTENTS

Postcards from the Supply Chain

Expat

Hinterlands

Postcards from the Supply Chain

Et puisque vous parlez d'usines et d'industries, ne voyez-vous pas, hystérique, en plein coeur de nos forêts ou de nos brousses, crachant ses escarbilles, la formidable usine, mais à larbins, la prodigieuse mécanisation, mais de l'homme, le gigantesque viol de ce que notre humanité de spoliés a su encore préserver d'intime, d'intact, de non souillé, la machine, oui, jamais vue la machine mais à écraser, à broyer, à abrutir les peuples?

— AIMÉ CÉSAIRE

Subduction Zone

On the sidewalk, a school of new bicycles
gleam like shiner sea perch. You've stepped in
to buy a pump or a tire. It is April. The sun
flutters hopefully behind the passing weather.

Darwin waits with me. Fiddling with the brakes
on a blue Norco road bike, he mentions again
that species evolve. Chuck! what good
does that do us now? We've argued this point

already. Remember the gas flares, Terminator gene,
Dolly, the imperatives of commerce. He nods,
slowly, and we gaze out at the thick city, an ocean
buoying exquisite glass diatoms, tiny

sea butterflies winging through its glinting
blue. I should have been frantic, there
at the edge of a fault, the Marianas
Trench. But how could I know?

Darwin, too, was blinded by the day, its varieties
of intricate machines. I couldn't guess
how it would haunt me, the ocean rolling on
and all of us swimming out into it.

Nine Meditations on Edward Burtynsky

GREAT SPHINX

Broad headdress fanned 'round the regal brow,
It gazes inland to Gangaridai's ancient cities,
Green hills smouldering in the day's last heat.

Beneath its lofty, rusted sternum—steel
Article of transoceanic faith—men, barefoot,
Shirtless in the russet mud, undo the hephaestic

Labour in this stripped, eroded monument
With their acetylene tools. Ah, commerce!
Gas lines coil like entrails on the sand.

*After "Shipbreaking #27, with Cutter, Chittagong,
Bangladesh"*

COLLOSEUM

Lions elephants bears and horses wild goats
deer and boars numbering nine thousand
fetched from throughout the empire
slain in one hundred days

of venationes and horse races, naval battles
three thousand strong, infantry combats, chariot races,
wild beast hunts and gladiatorial duels that marked
the hunting-theatre's dedication. At its close, Titus
wept bitterly for all to see and on the next sundown

died. Perhaps he shouldn't have
taken his brother's wife. History
isn't clear. In any case, by noon
his brother had claimed his title.

After "Mines #22, Kennecott Copper Mine,
Bingham Valley, Utah"

PYRAMIDS AT GIZA

But when Cheops took the throne,
they say, all Egyptians were made to abandon
their arts, their talents, their skills and trades
and give themselves to the labour
of stones, their quarrying and conveyance.

The Pharaoh dreamed a mountain
where none had been, a pinnacle
of imperial might, his immortality.

They brought the stones
from the range of Arabian hills,
across the Nile to the Libyan range beyond.
Ten years to build the causeway, twenty
for the pyramid itself, hundreds

of thousands of men. An inscription
records the quantity of onions, radishes, garlic
the labourers consumed.

After "Bao Steel #8, Shanghai, 2005"

TROJAN HORSE

The world made small by water.
Shipload on shipload

of war arrived at the coast. Grinding,
weathering them all. Now, at sunset, ships
gone home, they open the gates
to the beachhead, its rusted debris,
the scuffed-up battleground and then

the horse. It is mammoth. It looms.

A line of men, cables over their shoulders,
head out to reel it in: its high-arched shiplap neck,
the clinker-built belly, great
hewn-pine keel of its spine.

Tell me the whole truth. Why
raise up this giant, gleaming thing?

Bring it in! cried Thymoetes, who saw
not the last of the ships but a prize,
a gift of the kind, the generous gods.

After "Shipbreaking #8 Chittagong, Bangladesh"

STYX

You have left the low hills,
mute now with distance,

for barren ground. A stream glints
with whatever spirit moves water

from high and lonely places
in search of companionship,

never turning back. It reminds you
not to be hard, nor unsettled

in this absence of ancestors,
your part in the story uncertain

as it lies here burnt and trickling,
a sadder, broken thing

you cannot drink nor take
delight in. For its waters will eat

crystal and glass, copper and tin,
silver and pottery and flesh—things

you might once have brought it
to be livened, to be cleansed.

After "Nickel Tailings #34, Sudbury, Ontario"

HANGING GARDENS

I destroyed the city
and its houses, from foundation to parapet.
I devastated and I burned them.

I tore out the bricks
and earth of its walls, of its temples,
of the ziggurat—all that there was
I hove into the Euphrates. I dug canals

through that city, I drowned it.
I made its very foundations disappear.

I destroyed it more completely
than a devastating flood.

So that the city, its temples and gods,
would not be remembered, I blotted it out
with water. I made of it an inundated land.

And with the labourers I took, my spoil,
I raised up the palace at Kuyunjik. I cut
a canal through the arduous Mount Tas
to bring the waters of the Khosr, I watered

the meadows of the Tigris and planted gardens,
orchards with seeds gathered in the lands
I had conquered: pines, cypresses, junipers, almonds,

dates, ebony, ash, rosewood, olive, tamarik, walnut,
terebinth, fir, oak, pomegranate, pear, quince, grapevine,
fig. All that the gods had bestowed upon the earth

I arrayed in my palace without rival, amid streams
numerous as the stars of heaven. I gave it order, grace,
grandeur as befitted me, guardian of honour, lover
of justice, pious and charitable, with all humankind
submissive at my feet.

After "Feng Jie #4, Three Gorges Dam Project,
Yangtze River, 2002"

AQUEDUCT

Tot aquarum tam multis necessariis molibus
pyramidas videlicet otiosas compares aut cetera
inertia sed fama celebrata opera Graecorum?
  — SEXTUS IULIUS FRONTIUS, *De Aquaeductu*
    Urbis Romae

A city above all
must have water, public works
to ensure its supply. How beautiful

and how useless the pyramids,
the Mausoleum, the statue of Zeus.
Pretentious and fanciful, those empires

crumpled. We have annexed their lands.
We have engineered roads, conduits
that converge in imperial Rome,

their substructures and arches
traverse the valleys, the low-lying terrain.
Their tunnels perforate mountains.

No sight is more marvellous, no work
more enduring. We have laid
ten thousand miles of pipes.

After "Oil Fields #28, Cold Lake Alberta, Canada,
2001"

TAJ MAHAL

It rose like a lotus from the riverbank,
a great white blossom of his grief.

In the shadow of her absence, how he longed
for sovereignty over the world

of seclusion, but Divine Decree
had burdened him with care

of all humanity, its protection
and management, administration of all matters

pertaining to the common good.
Were he not charged with these

most pressing affairs of the Caliphate, great
pearls of sadness might have bowed him

but the helmsman of a glorious kingdom may not miss
a day attending to matters of state. For love of his wife

he raised the Taj, jewel of the empire,
inscribing on its funereal arch: Ye are

an ill omen to us; if ye desist not,
we will stone you.

*After "Oil Refineries #15, Saint John, New Brunswick,
Canada, 1999"*

ATLANTIS

Critias, when Timaeus had finished,
took his turn to speak. He spoke
of Athens as it had been long ago,
its citizens virtuous and bold.

In those days, said Critias, thick forests
cloaked the highlands. And the soil! None
could match what we possessed—crops
abundant, our pastures enviably rich.

When they bared the land,
the loam rolled into the sea.
What remains, said Critias,
is a body wasted by disease.

He spoke next of Atlantis, lost island
larger than Libya and Asia, of its citadel
and sons of Poseidon, its temples,
palaces, its gymnasia and canals.

High-minded, he said, they cared
nothing for wealth, their blood laced
with the gods'. But the divinity in them
faded. Their ambition grew.

Avarice—steely, dangerous—
tainted their minds. And a wound
opened in the blood-dark sea,
a cavernous throat that the land

slid into, smug waves
licking over the unnavigable mud.

The cries of the drowning Atlantans
streamed over the sea as it buried them.

Where would they have fled
in the vast, desert ocean? They had made war
with each nation, its lands, extracting
as they desired.

Critias sat looking down at his hands
that had grown old, thinking
on all that he knew and it saddened him.
He said, I am old. I am old, I am filled

with the enormity of things
that haven't yet passed from this world.

*After "Pivot Irrigation / Suburb South of Yuma,
Arizona, USA, 2011"*

Coal Trains

Nightly, coal-trains
thrusting through the soft spruce
wake us with their couplings, crash

and grate that shake the house and jingle
stacks of china in the cupboards. They slide in
whistling, mile-long, bound for the swelling economies of Asia

from mines—Bear Run,
Deer Creek—you'd want to visit
for the wildlife-viewing if not

industrial prowess. Production at an all-time high
bends the Midwest flatland into growth curves
prowled by trucks that dwarf the average

suburban house. What riches from an old swamp.
One hundred forty-five billion short tons waiting
to hump into the daylight. Fifty thousand

square miles seamed with wealth, land lying ready
ready, crying out! for development, YES
to Jobs! Grow Trade and the Economy! Those natural

resources return tenfold in containers from China's
gay markets. Cosco and Seaspan fetch our toasters
and t-shirts, handbags, sofas, Nikes, while our marine

bulk handling plant—furnished with technology,
Best of Its Kind!—ramps up for this burgeoning flow
of affordable goods. Daily, progress

cuts a graceful arc along the North Pacific
shipping lanes, while the mines, the trains,
the factories, loading docks

keep up their good work 24/7. Even this
otherwise quiet backwater of the unindustrious,
this unhurried thoroughfare and happy depot

of the boons of developed and developing states,
plays its own small part: lubing the tracks
to speed the twenty-five million tonne throughput

on its one-way journey skyward. Now there's
something to get fired up about! The sheer
power in each car surging past to the far-off engine

pumping out SO_x and good times: beach vacations,
GoreTex, all the little
party favours of the age.

Leaving the Mountains

Hands in the small warmth of pockets,
walk across the pebbled ground. Wind

whistles a tune through its teeth, icy,
dry. Flamingos have gathered at the lake,

lifting their wrought-iron legs. Smoke trails
from the mud-brick house near the shore

where a woman bakes flatbreads for her family
in a tiny stove lit with twisted shrubs.

Her llamas flick their ribboned ears,
gazing over the stone wall of the corral

to their pasture—knots of rock,
snow-streaked, tufted yellow grass. Mountains

tip their hard, wrinkled throats. Forget
living here. You will always be poor. Often

lonely. It makes this beauty much more
difficult to see.

La Granadilla

It is the season. An old woman without teeth
enters the café. She carries
a plaid canvas bag from which she takes the fruit,
placing it on the table, raising two fingers.
I pass the coin.

Later, on the terrace, sun
pressing itself against the mountainsides,
I take the granadilla in my palm. It is light
as an egg. I slice it with a pocket knife
and break open the golden rind

to foetal dawn, mist's
petals, sunrise
pearled in a rising sun. I taste
the smooth, sweet skins of sky,
black words breaking in the teeth.

Illness

All day I lie alone
in the stone hut
unable to eat,
drink, stand. Heat
rolls in, merciless.

Years after parting,
I still write
the unsent letters—
grateful, at such times,
for your company.

Cerro Rico

When the mountain has eaten
all the men they can feed it, they order more
from overseas and shovel those in too. Coal

firing an empire, they descend by thousands
to die underground. The crossed God stops
at the land's orifice and watches them go,

little boys slithering down capillaries
in the blasted rock, men losing themselves
to explosion and rock fall and bloom of dark gas.

They pickaxe down the muddy warrens,
hips and shoulders sticking in the squeezes
chewed through by water puckering cold

in stalactites overhead—cobalt bright, gleam
of cupric and sulphur in the rock-dusted air—
leaking into pools at their ankles and knees.

Corpses come up dust-shrouded and the living,
eyes bandaged against daylight, stagger out
hot and damp, heaving up baskets of ore.

Blue-skinned, bony, lungs rotted with dust,
they fall with fever in the mountain's thick frost
that Spain might make war with the Dutch.

Vorkuta

The locomotive galloped all night to arrive here, this desolate
platform brazen with frost. I have no suitcase. Only a memory
I've carried again and again out of the Kapitalnaia
with barrows of its coal: you on the steppe, an antelope

cantering under the sun that stooped to bless
the pious barley, all of us bending to the sheaves,
to scythes that whisked, bringing the grain to its knees.
And it seems now that there is no more sense

in what we did, in the wheat we cut and sheaved that summer
only to cut and stook again the following year, than there is
in the mine, but at least the end of the harvest brought gladness
to you and Oleg and the children, round-faced, golden.

The wind surges, blurring the world into a nether realm
of blue-white bones hemmed with frost, glass shards
that drive me to the steps of the train and I clutch the sun
in my mind like a torch, the only thing I might be sure

is not a dream. A small boy creeps near, his open hands
frostbitten, bare, feet wrapped in rags, the wire cage
of his body rattling in the wind.
I unbutton my coat and crouch to wrap him in it,

and his thin peaked face moves into what he thinks
joy might look like. He is almost correct,
though in truth, neither of us is moved by these gestures
we each perform out of necessity.

Thank You for Patiently Waiting

The technician is generous. I have certainly been waiting; I am not patient. A customer service rep patched me through a series of clicks and silences and seven minutes of soft rock and now he and I and my ailing computer are here together in the ether.

There is a delay in the connection so that time and again the technician and I start in at the same moment, stop, pause, talk over one another once again. Something's gone haywire and I haven't backed up in weeks! He is unruffled. *Yes ma'am don't worry we will fix it.* Sure. They aren't his files, not his problem. He speaks with a lilt and I wonder where I've wound up. Mumbai? Bangalore?

I don't ask. It would defy the industry ruse that the neighbourhood technician is just across town. Maybe he is, does it matter? Why complicate things. The cursor flits across the screen, prowling through menus and settings. I don't ask about his children or his parents, what it looks like outside his window, what time it is there and whether it is rainy or hot, how he slept, what he will eat today—none of the elemental human concerns that bridge every distance. He is busy doing his job and I am preoccupied with my files. *Ma'am?* His voice arrives clearly via binary code, translating the contraption that unites us.

Red List

Morning in that kitchen,
drying dishes was it? Tired,
your eyelid drooped, a pale leaf
under its petiole scar. We stepped out
into the garden. There may have been bees.

Everywhere, the forests go on dying.
If there were some way to gather up
the ashy thrush, the small-clawed otter,
the pittas, the narrow-mouthed toad,
I would bring them to you, one by one,
before the wind scatters them like milkweed.

How many creatures need your good heart!
Wait here, I will bring okapis, rhinos,
hawks. I will fetch a coiled black millipede,
thick and supple as a rope. The thousand
loose threads of its feet will carry it
out of my hands into yours.

Expat

1. A person working outside their own country, sometimes on a fat corporate contract, sometimes as a foreign expert, sometimes just as an English teacher.

2. A migrant, generally from an English speaking country, with more money and/or attitude than the average citizen.

— URBAN DICTIONARY

Arrival: Manila

midnight traffic north lane lane lane south lane lane
lane chock-a-block gridlock fighting cocks bumpered
up bus car jeepney truck taxi taxi moped car out
the windows billboard billboard mall mall mall
apartment blocks palm trees cola sellers office blocks
and three two one more block hotel parking lot street
vendors doughnuts mam mam doughnuts doughnuts
eating rice fish coke bright white fluorescent light
and sidewalks under doorways under staircases and
overpasses rodents and the cardboard bedsheets
sleeping little kids

The Work

*Whether or not your local colleagues wanted
you there in the first place, your first job is to
make them glad that you have arrived.*

New arrival from Manila, complete
with logframe, Gantt chart, outcomes,
alphabet soup accountability.
Desk in Forest Management alongside
thirty others. Myra types forms
on a Remington in triplicate,
Tata does payroll
with a pen, Edwin files it all
in banks of cabinets
that subdivide the hall,
its cheerful curtains drawn to help
the ramshackle A/C unit. Money
might have been more useful,
but a creature of higher
learning must possess
particular skill. Say,
an aerial view.

Evening

Late-day light drops its yellow leaves
on the village and the silver-tongued hills.
Placid carabaos muzzle the cropped grass.
From the canal a leggy water bird takes flight.

Roosted on the far hills, tall, backlit
clouds flash and rumble, coquettes.
Above, the sky all ruddy, mauve.
Bats appear. A star.

The dark, unleashed, stalks out of the undergrowth.
It creeps around the equable cows,
slips down from its nest in the palms, climbs
damply out of the creek. A nameless bird calls.

Wind stirs the cogon grass. The mountains,
the trees go, even the ground. The path, invisible,
cuts a line through the mind. It blurs and bleeds
into night's foreign plain.

Kin

Packed jeepney. Driver reaching back for coins. Passengers
on two long benches, third row down the middle,
back to back on stools set between the lines of knees.
Wise to cross yourself before you sit.

Wedged around me, three dozen others and a man,
twenty-something, tight jeans, black t-shirt, spiked hair,
a child sleeping on his lap. She leans
against him, but has nowhere to rest her head.

Outside, the moonlit ocean flashes through the trees.
The rusting jeepney, jolting, stops and starts, people
jostle out. Clatter of unmuffled engine.
Hot wind huffs through the cutaway walls.

The girl is three, maybe four, and sleeps
upright without stirring. The man holds her
with an arm around her waist—elbows out, awkward—
one slender steady hand cradling her face.

The Work

In March, the men went to the villages with clipboards and questionnaires the foreigner had prepared. The villagers were polite. They set aside their morning tasks—laundry, tending crops, hauling water, walking their carabaos to the shady streams, minding shops and small children, building and mending—and waited patiently in the shade for their turn to be questioned. Perhaps they were curious. Maybe they hoped to hear *what is it that you need?* There might be benefits of some kind. The men were also polite. Efficient. On the sheets they circled numbers, letters, marked down yes or no. They asked the assigned questions, check-marked the boxes and wrote a word or two where only many words could reasonably suffice. They cracked a few jokes that made everyone smile. When it was over, the villagers trailed home and the men drove by motorbike to the next place.

Island

Thin land, bare,
bony, exhausted,
its limestone knuckles up
through a skiff of shabby grass.
Scrubby trees panhandle,
collecting plastic trash. Tethered cows—
thin, long-neglected garden tools—
rake at the stubble.

In the village they have captured a manta ray
and now flense its starry arms
outside the huts. Along the gunwales
and the outriggers of fishing boats,
strips of meat hang drying. Smoke
curdles like hot albumin around
the yolky sun. Out on the beach, its stink
settles into my clothes. Oh

to swim out! past the pale reef
into the blue purity of sea and sky.
But a fish—long
as a machete and swift—
rips through the shallows.
The little wrasse leaps up,
stranding itself on shore.

Labourers

On the jeepney roof ten bags of cement,
three labourers, fat rebar bundles jutting fore and aft.
At the corner before the climb, the shiftless hillside
has dropped a new fan of rubble on the road.

Far below, a river folds itself into the fields,
into the shadows of the steep green hills.

Three miles over this mountain to the village—
up the switchbacked road, down precipitous steps
to the footpath sidewinding around the hill.
Hopping down, I shoulder my pack and go.

Behind, the labourers unload
rebar, the cement. They heave the sacks
onto one another's backs,
lime clouding at the seams.

A little way up, I pause to let them muscle past,
panting, slick, slogging their burdens upslope.

Tappia Falls

Early morning. Across the terraced gold bowl
of the stonewalled fields, down the steep trail
to the falls—no one. The path drops
into deep-throated gorge, sweet
hullabaloo of green, its extravagance—undergrowth,
overgrowth piled and twining, tresses
laid over the rocks, lianas dripping tangled
in sheets down the cliffs. And water! Water
chutes over its bedrock, olive green
plunging and licking up whitely, its wind
lifting ferns up the canyon's
slick walls, wet air levers the spray,
mist surges and roils, uplifted
by the water's sheer drop. It comes down
plumed, roaring, veiled and gentle, tasting
of its secret headwaters, the high-up places,
unsullied, sunlit, unknown, unseen.

The Work

In the evenings, I write out the new words.
By day, transcribe them onto the landscape.

Kahoy: tree
Bukid: mountain
Bugas: rice
Ulan: rain

Init: hot
Kaayo: very
Lisod: difficult
Wala: none

Morning Jog

Each morning at daybreak the man jogs slow laps of the basketball court. He wears sneakers and blue track pants with yellow stripes down the legs. When he sees me round the bend in the dusty lane, he bounces in place beneath the line of breadfruit trees until I reach him and we jog together as far as the first bridge. Then he says, "Let's walk now." He used to be stronger but has grown old. Seventy. If he were young, he would run *fast!* all the way to Putloncam! It pains him, not to be able to run so far now. But at this sensible speed he can greet the neighbours tending their orchids, their potted spurges. He waves as we pass and they gibe about his new pastime. Other things, too, best to ignore. At the second bridge, I trot on ahead, up one small hill then the next, between the pastures past grazing cattle and farmers whose heads swivel as I pass. And then I turn back, slowing to a walk as I reach him. We return to the junction and he lopes toward his home and I turn back to the rented house. "See you tomorrow!" he cries, lifting his hand. "Yes, tomorrow," though I've never asked for company. It's 6:30 now, the day already searing.

Reef

Drop into the sovereign blue.
It takes your weight

like an ingot in its palm,
considering. Very well,

jackfish!— three storeys
of the finest silver plates.

A vat of indigo,
quicksilver-spliced, blennies

school among the parapets
pillars, polyps. Ruffed

and quilled, a lionfish
to promenade you down

the hanging garden's wall
past its minarets and friezes,

chiaroscuro and statuary,
ostentatious, baroque!

But what of words?

Glassy nothings
gasped, flitting off.

Market

This morning one of the market kittens
lay down to die. Its curled body rests
in a corner at the bottom of the steps,
beneath the table of foot-long beans
and sari sari vegetables. Its little head

lies slightly sideways, one ear flattened,
chin tipped up, an incisor just visible
below the lip. Its whole body slumps
over the bone undercarriage,
a heap of twigs beneath its fur.
Dear kitten, how sweetly
death called to you, stroking
your xylophone ribs, little ginger throat.

It is early. The vendors
of fruit and dried fish have just risen.
They put away their bedding and wash
at the tap. A woman rounds up bits of trash
with a dustpan, a worn palmyra broom.

Levee

Breezing along the land's ridge cap, red levee road,
helmetless, leaning the curves. Blurred world slurs past,
blousy clouds flouncing over, and the rice paddies—flooded,
    brilliant
with seedlings and late afternoon sun—flash silver, brown,

slender green. We chase yesterday's rain gush
down the concrete canal, past white-shirted children,
goats tethered in the roadside shade. In the valley far
beyond, below, more fields chequer the lowlands lifting

smoothly into peaks that nudge the distant sky: pinions, or
vertebrae of starved cats. Land's fabric, threadbare,
draped over them. Think Brahmin cattle
and their hanging hides. Dewlaps. Lizard's wattle.

Decades ago, machines arrived
to scrape the hillsides clean. They peeled back
towering diptero-
carps, mottled *Rafflesia*, rhinoceros beetles round and

shiny as spoons, the rolling pin
millipedes, butter-
flies that live nowhere else. They
swallowed

the hornbills, the
barbets, the blue-
throated bee-
eaters,

shaded
hollows and their
leopard
cats,

and shat out
the bones, shards
of coral rock sprouting
hot cogon grass, cobras. Rain,
washing over, scours out its little souvenirs.

Under the unfettered sun,
heat:
an iron cage with no door.

Scalded

At home, winter.
Dim, impenetrable days.
But here? Fiercest
month of the year, sun
lances down murderous,
glancing off the glossed palms,
wilting the languid bananas.

Swimming out
from rocks carpeted with urchins—
where to step? Breakers,
shore, sun, all furious. By nightfall

the skin is slow-spit-roasted,
gut studded with landmines.
Body pilloried, the spirit falls out,
and hair, too, day by day,
fistfuls.

But the breeze-lifted curtains.

The coltish palms.

Swallows in the mossed cathedral,
and the moonlit canticles of banyan.

The Work

An old man from the village, writing:
Tungod kay daghan ang mga illegal loggers, daghan
na mga kalamidad sama sa baha, landslide ug huwaw
tungod kay na upaw na ang nga kalasangan dakung
epekto sa mga mag-uuma.

There are many illegal loggers and many calamities—
floods, landslides and scarcity—because the hills are
denuded. This has great effects on the rice farmers.

The young man beside him who waited for the pen:
Ang kahimtang namo karon lisod kaayo kay dili na
makapamotol wala kahoy. Kay dakpon man mao
untay among paninguha an ang pag baligya sa kahoy
arong ang ipalit ug bugas.

Our situation now is very difficult because we can no
longer cut down trees—they will arrest us. It is our
livelihood, selling trees to buy rice.

Cockpit

The neighbour's five cockerels, chained
at the ankles, peck Venn diagrams
of all possible logical relations. Attentive
to duty (in fact, OCD), they herald
each morning two hours before it arrives.
My cinder block bedroom, echo chamber
in turquoise, amplifies their mighty din.

I have high hopes for the cocks. At 4 a.m.,
may they will go one by one *sa bowangan*,
to the cockpit down the hill,
and lose. I pray for an occasion
honourable enough to mark
with a feast. Chicken
adobo, *lechon* chicken, *hinalang
na manok. Gigutom na ko!*

The chickens, their shrieks, break open
the morning to rhythmic metallic on metal.
Crouched shirtless on his lawn, Eddy
mows with a pair of large and rusted shears.
His cigarette dangles. The cocks
twitch their royal heads. His wife Dinah
stands rocking the baby, her little boy,
maybe three, playing at her feet.
She is twenty-three. Her black hair
falls all the way down her back, thick
as a forest, a waterfall at night.
Later Eddy brings the nets.
They mend them together on the grass.

❖

Cockpit, a weekly spectacle,
Sundays after church.

Some men, some vendors of snacks
doze on benches in the shade.

Under the tin roof a man stitches shut
the wounded bird lolling in his lap.

Tiers of packed benches ring the pit,
its rust-stained floor, its drifting feathers.

Fingers bristling folded bills, the kristo
gathers bets. The referee brings the birds,

sets them down to circle, flush up,
lunge with bladed legs—once,

63

thrice, and slump to the planks, ready
enough to die. But the ref scoops them up,

riles them. There's life left here,
and money still to change hands.

After midnight. A fat moon lounges in the sky,
tossing dice across the bay. It runs its hands
over the manes of palms that shift like mules in a corral.
The fishermen are out, Eddy and the others. At dawn
they haul up the slender, outriggered boats.

Their wives are there to meet them, to lay the catch
on tables along the road. Small tuna mostly,
the odd skate, plenty of reef fishes: fat and pink,
square-headed, silver, their bodies piled and sliding.
Steadily less plentiful, yet all of us go on eating.

❖

Full-blown day thrusts itself on us
sticky-hot, laced with salt. We retreat
to our shaded homes. Bougainvillea
erupts over the fences. In the gardens

orchids, euphorbs, opulent hibiscus
nod prettily at the washboard sky. Dinah
has been absent all week. Her mother-in-law
on the patio bench jigs the baby on her knee,

the little boy swings his feet.
To Canada, she says. Very cold.
There are homes for the aged, many
children in need of good care.

The Work

Respondents 1 through 48:
these times it's hard the harvest was bad very hot
weather frequent typhoons we need work lack of
water lack of job it's hard now faced with crises and
very hot weather unemployment there's no work
commodities are expensive many are jobless we're
faced with problem of climate change when it rains
our crops are flooded and when it's hot it's so hot our
plants wither it would be nice if there's livelihood
there's a problem of income it's not enough for the
family now it's hard people should help one another
so that there's a little progress problems with lack
of food lack of water resources our situation now is
hard we need finances so much hard work we have
problems with water crisis of expenses not enough
livelihood people need finances and food crisis need
food really very hard rice is expensive there's little
water no money problems of employment problem of
lack of food it's hard due to hot weather we didn't have
a good harvest our livelihood is affected problems
with water and hard to find food our situation is very
hard now we don't have potable water it's very hard
because of problems with water and very hot weather
we're having problems finding livelihoods no rain and
no work we didn't have a good harvest very hard for

us farmers because we're practicing three croppings and we didn't have a good harvest due to floods it's hard because it's very hot we don't have potable water it's hard to find money we have a problem on water and the surroundings are dirty trash is thrown anywhere malnutrition lack of education especially on cleaning the surroundings it's hard now rice and copra are expensive no jobs there's a lack of sources of livelihood and water and food problem of water it's very hard commodities are expensive and there's no permanent job our condition is a little difficult because of low income there's problems with water we are thankful to God for our good health there's lack of food and water maybe lack of prayer it's hard because there's lack of food problem of livelihood the environment is no longer sustainable very hard because there's less catch in the river problem of water and everyday needs and food and the very hot weather it's very hard there's no money to support our families we're having a problem on water rice finances   in other words it's hard

Pump in the Yard

The girls from up the hill have finished
laundering in basins at the tap in our yard,
last in the neighbourhood to give water.
Their cooking fires smudge the noon air.

The rain we've waited weeks for arrives
briefly this afternoon, washing the sweat
from the broad black backs of the carabaos
who swish their tails in delight. I've had

plenty of ideas about things—about water,
about hard work. Men hurry out to break
the stubbled fields, heaving ploughs
behind their animals, ankle deep in muck.

I watch them out the kitchen window, filling
my kettle at the sink, turning on the gas.

Ants

In the two days of my absence, a string of ants
arrives in the kitchen to carry away the rice.

They jawed open the plastic sack and now heft it, grain
by grain, under the shelf along the counter to the window.

They ignore my arrival, working steadily until
my sticky buns, mangoes, coax them past the sink

in red knots, swarming. Their little hearts
swell at my offerings. They have never run

faster, worked harder. Their holes in the walls
bloom semicircles of sand. I inform the landlady.

She arrives with the spray.

After that, the apartment goes quiet. I leave fish bones
in the sink with impunity. Day after day, my own company.

The neighbour in the facing house, elderly and ill,
dies in the night. Someone strings a tarp

across the road, sets out tables, chairs.
Well-wishers crowd the street. They sit me down

and offer Beer na Beer with Coke. Small kids
race around on bikes and the priest arrives

to say the blessings. The crowd grows
all evening, filling the street loudly,

more food, more beer, singing, prayers.
I watch from behind my curtain.

At dawn, cockerels. Whisky bottles
on the table, three men lounging in the chairs,

a breeze and their lingering voices softly
billow the curtain, filling the quiet room.

❖

For ten days the street is an impassable clatter,
voices jangling into the night. I fall asleep late

to laughter and Mah Jong tiles shuffled,
wake to the same sounds. Five days in,

the ants return. Penitent, they creep around
the edges of the room, grabbing morsels

off the floor. I drop larger crumbs, listening
to the throngs outside. The late neighbour's daughter,

a schoolteacher in Davao, waits for a leave.
The priest returns. I lose track of days

but soon the ants, *hormigas*, *amigas*,
disappear again. All evening, nothing.

Again the next day. I crouch
near the sand piles, cajoling the wall.

At last the daughter arrives.
They bury the neighbour.

They put away the tables and stash the tarp.
Litter and beer bottles linger on the roadsides

and a son or a nephew moves into the house.
Life continues as before. I go out

to get bread. I go out like a teenager
in a growth spurt, everything ill-fitting, strange words

gangly in my mouth. I collect
glances, whispers; waves

of conversation part before me, closing as I pass.
In the evenings, sometimes,

the tiniest black ants. Larger brown ones. Going on
around my comings, goings

as if I wasn't there.

Hinterlands

My Lord, I am Delgamuukw. I am a Gitxsan Chief and a plaintiff in this case. My House owns territories in the Upper Kispiox Valley and Upper Nass Valley. Each Gitxsan plaintiff's House owns similar territories. Together, the Gitxsan and Wet'suwet'en Chiefs own and govern the 22,000 square miles of Gitxsan and Wet'suwet'en territory. For us, the ownership of the territory is a marriage of the Chief and the land. Each chief has an ancestor who encountered and acknowledged the life of the land. From such encounters come power. The land, the plants, the animals and the people all have spirit, they all must be shown respect. That is the basis of our law.

— DELGAMUUKW V. BRITISH COLUMBIA
Proceedings of the Supreme Court, May 12 1987

Accessory

When fall came, I was not the one to rest
the tip of the .22 on the broad forehead

of one trusting hog after another. I did not squeeze.
I stood ready to pass the sticking knife

and I pinned the pig down as it lurched
and kicked the air. I did not draw the knife

through the throats of thirty-six
roosters. I drew out their sodden feathers,

their slick entrails, the stiff, spent windpipes
that squawked. I held the bobbing pig under

and it scalded. Red-handed, I scraped. I hung
its headless hairless carcass to cure.

And when all that—thank God—was over,
I was still whole, untainted

by that dark thing that might dwell in me. Death
was in my hands but not of them. I dealt

with death, but did not deal it. I stood beside it,
watching, making what good I could of its offal.

And yet. All winter I served the farm dog
severed heads and feet. I ate their cleaned

and butchered bodies. And there was
no distance, no difference.

Umshewa

Again I walked the canyon's rim in order
not to think. White sat fat on the land, black dactyl
creeks, rivers breaking through.
                              I had bludgeoned

each uncertainty with logic, intellect, those blunt
weapons. Their measured, hyperbolic words
dice shaken in a loose fist. My learning,
                              heavy

bundle of sticks. Hemlocks bent
under their snow load—mind
coasting its tired track—and the raw air
                              knifed in,

pivoting bare aspens that stroked the lovelorn
grey sky. Everywhere, winter stood, gaunt nostalgia
mewing at its ankles.
                    Below,

ice leaned over the passing water, thrusting
blue knees into the sleek dark. Night
had ebbed just enough to expose

this small rock of noon. I was riddled
with thinking, with the thought of our time,
wormed, eaten.
      What small husk

remained to see the world? Blind
heart, it burrowed into human knowing
that had drifted here from elsewhere.

D11 Cat

Beyond the mind's flight—circumscribed
by gravity, grammar, Descartes—a fiasco of poplars
lift stippled hands to the clean October sky.
Resplendent, they have almost finished speaking.
They stand together below the honeyed

sacrificial ridge, its burnished throat laid bare.
In the yellow autumn air four grizzlies
root through the undergrowth. Water trickles
down a fan of scree into the ground becoming

its sinews, arteries, lungs—and the land
sinks into your subterranean mind,
the cavernous space there, brightness
surging through. The stone sheep
that starts at your scent and canters off, its breath
hanging in the air as you arrive where it stood.
That is your wonder made real.

Go there. And go at once. By daybreak,

this mountain will be Cat tracks.
Someone else's job.

April

Blue, blue and the slapdash clouds—clouds
burled up over the buckled ridge. Limelight
fell through the naked windows of my eyes.

We skinned toward the spiny peak, across
the boilerplate wind-slab, sun-broken cornice
ominous above, toward its many-named face,

a granite altar scoured, fissured, polished by time,
by tongues that have praised it, empty hands
pressed against it, extended for its alms.

In the lockjawed rock, a vein
of ancestry, fault line of migration,
our story. Landfall.

Trapline

A high fog, pearl-grey and lifting; clear
sky peers through, blue. Overnight,
white air alighted on each thing.
Each twig sprouts white thorns. White
fringes the clinging leaves—curled,
brown, edges aflame with cold.
He goes out to check the line.

Clouding up underfoot, snow, its attic
of small treasures, legible movements
of invisible, intersecting lives. Five miles
from the cabin, he kneels
in the wreckage of snow that clots
on his mittens, furring the slender mink

that he pries from the Conibear. Lifting it
to meet his breath, the fine-point crystals
weep into its pelt and he touches his cheek
to the almost-alive fur, its fine, hidden bones.

Snow arrives. It lays an arm across his shoulders
its breath cold in his ear. And the snowflakes
go on gathering, whispering
among themselves.

Weight

The boot-crunch of snow says it.
I have grown old. Stopping, silence

rises all around. My breath
lifts and dies in the frozen air.

Across the river two horses,
shaggy, bend to their tattered bale,

the lone warm figures
on this grey and bluish land.

I would go to them,
thawing as they idled over

unhurried, curious, to snuffle
at my hands for apples, grain—

but the black river
roils between us.

I lie down beside it.
It covers me with stones.

Milking

It is early evening, it is already dark,
when someone comes to the gate

with the blue rope, the halter. Together
they cross the yard to the barn.

There is the grain. There, the glow
of a bare bulb falling through the half-door

on the scaled, blown snow.
There is the frosty stantion's clank.

A shoulder against her rumen.
A forehead, cheek. That snuffling

breath clouding the dim air,
warm hands underneath, tugging,

then the hollow, tinny jet
of milk on metal and she shifts

her weight, the calf kicking.
She glances behind

at the stooped back, the knees
gripping the cold pail. This one

is sad again. She is sorry.
She has given what she can.

Sleeping Out

Night. The moose stepped up. I woke where I lay
on the moss and our gazes met, caesural.
What I was then: lifted: wind breathed through
the dewy webs of thought and broke them.

And then afraid. Petrified by night,
its strangeness, inscrutable inhumane
mountains, the freshet creek and its language
no human ear can know. I closed

my eyes. Rain rode in, sharp hooves
dashing over the tarpaulin. Again, thought,
fearful, hammered in my mind's pipes—
an airlock stuck behind the walls.

It was too much to be alone with,
all this wild. My mind still framed
with the houses I had built there,
rooms I haven't found my way out of.

Fourth Law of Ecology

The sun doesn't lift the yellow hand
it has laid on your back. Summer heat

rises from the blonde sweep of grass
to a hawk drawing circles on the liquid sky.

The rabbit, snared, sees the hawk. It feels
your footsteps thump down the wire, taut

and blameless as hunger,
as greed.

Burning off

First the old grass—matted, drab, unclothed
by the resolute sun. The line of flame
charges like a light brigade.

He watches it gallop, its eager skirmish
flaring in the wind, its snicker at the grass.
It meets the road and falters,

and he crosses the scorched earth to heap
branches from the fence line, pour
the gasoline. He brings the box and tosses on

sheaves of letters, notebooks
that smoke at the margins, catch.
Heat carries their soft leaves,

brittle, blackened,
into the afternoon sky and the tired brush leaps,
magnificent.

Sunset

Evening light rose-gold on the spruce, sunset
and I lie back to admire the Ming dynasty sky.

Bees hum around us in the clover, making good
on obligations, keeping everything on track.

But the river roars, far off. Wind traipses about
wherever it wants, roguish, seeing things.

Soon the aspens will drop everything
and turn to their Trappist contemplation,

trusting in the order of things. They must.
Will they feel as I do at the sound of the cranes?

August

Huckleberries
wildly I ate you
lifting

each nippled fruit
from its green home
with my curious tongue

I was a bear
I was
ptarmigan

alive on the hellebore slope
breathing
the coalescing mist

small summer
rain descending desiring only
you

On Bikes

It's best begun on bicycles,
flying no-hands down a hill, wind
in your hair, your mouths, your open palms,
filled with heady abnegation of despair

for the human race, the mountain
ranges of its mind, its preoccupations and ordeals,
exist first, last, best in giddy two-wheeled careening,
in knee-pistoning glory, in a moment forever

summer, cut flowers and peaches on the table
of a kitchen still ringing long after the breathless
conversations have trailed off
into the sunlit room upstairs.

New Season

The last day of summer, she knocks down
the old chimney and carries the bricks outside.
Now the house is open to the sky.

She patches it
with an old blue tarp but the wind
lifts the edges and slides in anyway,
making itself at home. Each evening,

leaning against the counter,
the same expectant
bowl of fruit. Seated at the table,
the same salt.

But at the back door, someone
else's shoes. Everything blossoms,
the quiet air laden with its scent.

Nocturnes

The rain is tenacious. Intermittent all day, it falls through sunlight from an almost clear sky. Swallows lark about. Its downy fingers play arpeggios over their wings.

In from the autumn meadow
I build a fire in the oil-drum stove. Boots in the heat, drying the cuffs of my pants while darkness
snuffs out the far, the middle distance. Tousled blonde moon steps out from behind the hills.

All afternoon, the field. Grass rustles overhead.

We let the beer cool in the brook and the sun
butter our skin. I lie gazing up
at you and the sky that leaks summer,

geese calling out their valedictions.

The evening is filled with moths

needing to be carried outside. Hold them lightly
and their tracery wings, the silver feathers, suffer no injury.

More commonly, the startled moths, trapped
by the light, their captors, struggle, leaving the fingers

dusted with their breakage.

Under the pines, the soil's thin, scabbed. Fireweed
hasn't bloomed. Midway through the effort the small
plants died, leaves gone fuchsia,
stiff in summer's last breeze.

Wind follows its worn route.

Wind
gestures and the trees lean to see what it sees. Do they
see me? Whispering, they know.

I've stepped into the river of someone else's life.
My own flows on without me, somewhere else.

Until sunset, I'd held my hand against the low, brilliant sun.
Now your slender fingers on the piano, Chopin's Nocturne,
    E minor. Night
opens the door to listen, its undressing hands laying us bare.

It drops aspen-gold coins on the threshold. For the eyes,
the tongues of our love.

A trill of sleet already
on the air. Cranes
muster overhead,
spiralling.

This was to have been
the perennial tale,
this flyway,
this place.

They cry out to one another in their parting.
High, trumpeting calls.

Was it your name that clanged in my mind, a church bell?
The petals of your fingertips on my shoulders?

Or was it only rain.

NOTES

The opening epigraph by José Rizal is taken from his 1887 novel *Noli mi tangere* that exposed the corruption and despotism of the Spanish ruling class during its three hundred year occupation of the Philippines. It reads, "Let us not ask for miracles. Let us not ask for concern with what is good for the country of him who comes as a stranger to make his fortune and leave." Rizal is a Philippine national hero whose words and actions inspired the revolutionary activities that ended the Spanish colonial period. He was executed at the age of thirty-five.

Postcards from the Supply Chain

The epigraph is from Aimé Césaire's *Discours sur le colonialisme*, Présence Africaine, Paris, 1955.

Edward Burtynsky is a renowned Canadian photographer whose work documents the industrial sublime. The photographs referred to are published in the following books:

Manufactured Landscapes, National Gallery of Canada/ Yale University Press, 2003: "Mines #22, Kennecott Copper Mine, Bingham Valley, Utah" and "Nickel Tailings #34, Sudbury, Ontario."

China, Steidl, 2005: "Shipbreaking #27, with Cutter, Chittagong, Bangladesh," "Bao Steel #8, Shanghai, 2005," "Shipbreaking #8 Chittagong, Bangladesh" and "Feng Jie #4, Three Gorges Dam Project, Yangtze River, 2002."

Oil, Steidl, 2009: "Oil Fields #28, Cold Lake Alberta, Canada, 2001" and "Oil Refineries #15, Saint John, New Brunswick, Canada, 1999."

Water, Steidl, 2013: "Pivot Irrigation/Suburb South of Yuma, Arizona, USA, 2011."

Most of these images can also be viewed at edwardburtynsky.com.

The fifth stanza of "Trojan Horse" is adapted from a passage in Robert Fagles's translation of Virgil's *The Aeneid*, Viking Press, 2006.

Pausanias (c. CE 110 – CE 180) in his *Guide to Greece* discusses the Stygian stream that emerges from the ground at Nonakris, stating "its water is death to men and to all animals...The water of the Styx dissolves glass and crystal and agate and all the stone objects known to man, even pottery vessels. The water corrupts horn and bone, iron and bronze and even lead and tin and silver and the alloy of silver and gold." Translated by Peter Levi, Penguin Books, 1971.

"Hanging Garden" describes the sack of Babylon by King Sennacherib of Assyria in 689 BCE and the subsequent construction of the magnificent hanging gardens at his palace in Nineveh (where recent scholarship has found that this wonder of the ancient world was located, not in Babylon as popularly supposed). Much of the text is adapted from passages in "The Bavian Inscriptions." Translated from the cuneiform by Daniel David Luckenbill in *The Annals of Sennacherib*, University of Chicago Press, 1924.

The epigraph of "Aqueduct" reads: "With these grand structures, so numerous and indispensable, carrying so many waters, who indeed would compare the idle Pyramids or other useless, although renowned, works of the Greeks?" Translated by R.H. Rodgers, University of Vermont.

"Taj Mahal" is inspired by original Mughal texts collected in *Taj Mahal: The Illuminated Tomb: An anthology of seventeenth-century Mughal and European documentary sources*. Compiled and translated by W.E. Begley and Z.A. Desai (The Aga Khan Program for Islamic Architecture, Harvard University and the Massachusetts Institute of Technology; distributed by University of Washington Press, Seattle and London).

Vorkuta was the administrative headquarters for a network of Soviet gulags near the Arctic coast of the USSR.

Cerro Rico is the conical red mountain that towers over the town of Potosí in the Bolivian Andes. Beginning in the 1500s, an estimated two million enslaved indigenous South Americans and Africans lost their lives while extracting the silver that bankrolled the Spanish empire for three hundred years.

The IUCN Red List catalogues plant and animal species at risk of global extinction.

Expat

The Filippino voices in this section are speaking Cebuano, one of over 170 languages and dialects spoken in the archipelago.

The epigraph for "The Work" is taken from Ruth Stark's guide *How to Work in Someone Else's Country*, University of Washington Press, 2011.

Hinterlands

The Delgamuukw trial, initiated in 1984 by the Gitxsan and Wet'suwet'en nations, established aboriginal title as the right to the land itself rather than simply rights to its usage. Following ten years of trials and appeals, the Supreme Court ruled that the oral histories of Canada's first peoples are admissible as legal evidence for their claim to the land.

"Umshewa" (OOm-shwa) is a Gitxsan word meaning driftwood, commonly a slur for a white person.

ACKNOWLEDGEMENTS

For their kindness, hospitality and ongoing work on behalf of the lands, creatures and communities of Bohol many thanks are due to the staff at the Department of Environment and Natural Resources, the Bohol Environment Management Office and the Carood Watershed Management Council in Candijay, Carmen and Tagbilaran City, Philippines.

"Accessory" was previously published in *Contemporary Verse 2*; a previous version of "Vorkuta" appeared in *Arc Poetry Magazine*. Earlier versions of "Umshewa," "D11 Cat," "April," and "Sleeping Out" appeared on the Canada Writes portion of the CBC website. My thanks to the editors and publishers involved.

My thanks also to the Canada Council for the Arts and the BC Arts Council whose generous funding provided uninterrupted time to work on this manuscript. Scholarships from the Banff Centre for the Arts and Hollyhock along with retreats generously hosted by Bill Mix made it possible for me to work in some truly extraordinary places.

Karen Solie, Daljit Nagra, Jen Hadfield and Dionne
Brand all contributed valuable insights during the 2013
Banff Centre Writing Studio. I am also grateful to Brian
Huntington and Catriona Sandilands for their thoughtful
readings of the manuscript and to Beth Follett for her
work guiding this and so many other books into the
world. Thanks to Erica Gajewski for her work to capture
on paper and canvas some of the vanishing creatures
of the world and her permission to reproduce it here.
Most humble thanks to Jan Zwicky for her musical
ear and editorial savvy, her patience with lousy Skype
connections and her unfailing encouragement and
support.

Finally, this book would not have come into being
without the generosity of friends and family who tended
burst pipes, collected mail, fed the cat, and shipped,
received, sorted and stored many boxes of stuff over the
past several years. This book is for all of you, but most
especially for Jane and Tim McGiffin. I can't thank you
enough.

DANI COUTURE

Emily McGiffin's first poetry collection, *Between Dusk and Night*, was a finalist for the Raymond Souster Award and the Canadian Authors' Association Poetry Award. She is currently a PhD student in the Faculty of Environmental Studies at York University in Toronto.